From East to West

with Lewis & Clark

BY DEBORAH HEDSTROM

ILLUSTRATIONS BY SERGIO MARTINEZ

mw

MY AMERICAN JOURNEY
FROM EAST TO WEST WITH LEWIS & CLARK

My American Journey Series published by Questar Publishers
© 1996 by Questar Publishers

Illustrations © 1996 by Sergio Martinez

International Standard Book Number: 1-57673-066-2

Design by D² DesignWorks

Printed in Mexico

For information:
QUESTAR PUBLISHERS, INC.
POST OFFICE BOX 1720
SISTERS, OREGON 97759

97 98 99 00 01 — 10 9 8 7 6 5 4 3 2 1

19.99

Foreword

Captains Meriwether Lewis and William Clark really took the journey you will read about in this book. Everything happened just as it is written. We know this because the captains kept journals of their travels. And since we want you to experience Lewis' and Clark's adventures just as they did, this book is written like a journal. (The real journals are almost two hundred years old! They are carefully and safely stored in the American Philosophical Society in Philadelphia.)

Though the captains wrote down their experiences, they did not try and record every word spoken or thought. So I filled in these missing details by adding some imagination to the facts. I also added one other fictional part to this book. Paul Hale, or "Sparrow Hawk," is not a real person who went on the journey with Lewis and Clark. He is a character added just for fun. But the rest of the crew is real.

So get set for a true adventure — eat bear steaks, meet Indian tribes, and survive the wilderness of America's early west. And if you listen carefully, you may even hear the dock boards creak as the crew load supplies, and the Missouri River lap ripples against the bottom of their keelboat.

DEBORAH HEDSTROM

Introduction

Lash those barrels to the barge!

"Careful with that wooden box!

"Oh...you're here. You must be Paul Hale? I was so busy getting things ready for the trip that I did not notice your arrival. Captain Clark and I are glad to have you as our assistant. Stash your gear on the dock. Then I will tell you your duties and introduce you to the crew.

"First off, welcome to President Jefferson's Corps of Discovery. I have to admit you're a bit young, but I faced my first Indians when I was only ten. I noticed a fire left burning when the townspeople were hiding from a war party. Young people can be very observant, and we need that.

"But you didn't come to hear about my childhood. You'll be wanting to hear about our trip — the first scientific expedition across this land of America. The president is convinced that someday it will all be part of a single nation. He's the one who persuaded Congress to put up the twenty-five hundred dollars for our journey.

"I'm Captain Meriwether Lewis. The red-haired man on the barge is Captain William Clark. The two of us are in command. The trip from St. Louis to the Pacific Ocean requires working together, and doing what you are told is vital if we are to get back alive.

"Pardon me a moment.

"Hey! Back that wagon up to the dock.

"Clark, here's the load of tallow you wanted.

"Sorry. Where was I? That's right, your duties. As a scientific journey, we will do more than explore. We'll keep journals, draw maps, and collect samples of new plants, birds, and animals. The going will be rough and dangerous, and we will probably run low on food and clothes. But it will be the adventure of a lifetime.

"Let me introduce you to a few of the crew. Clark, this is our new assistant."

The red-haired man offered a friendly greeting. "Welcome! Good to see a young person joining us. Why, I was fighting redcoats with my big brother, George, when I was about your size. I understand you can read. That's real fine. We need good minds, as well as strong backs. The 1800s are bringing changes, and I figure we'll be a part of them! But I best stop jawing and get back to work, or we won't go anywhere. See you later."

Captain Lewis continued with his introductions. "The black man carrying the load of tallow is Clark's servant, York. The French boatman checking out the barge is Pierre Cruzatte. He claims he is the best boatman east of the Mississippi. We will have plenty of opportunities to find out on this trip!

"The soldier with his sleeves rolled up, and wearing suspenders, is Sergeant Charles Floyd. Most of his men will only be with us for the first part of our journey. President Jefferson sent them to help us through the Missouri River Indian territory. There's been a sight of trouble out that way.

"The big dog sleeping under the wagon is mine. I call him Scannon. No need to fear him. He's well behaved.

"That gives you enough to go on for now. I need to check the medical supplies Dr. Rush sent. Don't forget to sign the journey list, and we'll see you back here at dawn."

ST. LOUIS, MISSOURI, APRIL 1804

Journey List

George Drouillard	Ebenezer Tuttle
York	John Ordway
Toussaint Charbonneau	Nathaniel Pryor
Sacajawea	George Shannon
Patrick Gass	John Potts
John Colter	Francis Labiche
Pierre Cruzatte	Alexander Willard
Reuben Fields	George Gibson
Joseph Fields	Joseph Whitehouse
Hugh McNeal	Isaac White
John Shields	William Bratton
Charles Floyd	John Collins

Chapter One

INTO THE WILDERNESS

West of St. Louis, on the Missouri River, September 11, 1804

We're not the same crew that the people in St. Louis lined the shores to cheer and wave good-bye to. We've been on the Missouri River now for four months, and most of our spit and polish is gone. Sergeant Floyd was right when he told Private Tuttle not to let the cheering go to his head. "You won't be a real hero until you get back!" Floyd said.

This river sure doesn't make the getting forward easy! It's nothing like the Ohio and Mississippi Rivers that Lewis floated to get the keelboat from Pittsburgh to St. Louis. This river plagues us like a nightmare. The water rushes past, caving in banks and tossing around whole fallen trees as if they were mere twigs. We constantly dodge floating logs, buried snags, sand bars, and sudden shallows.

Going upriver makes for hard rowing and leaves the men with blisters and boils on their hands. Broken towropes force anyone who can swim to jump into the swift, muddy water. Often, only quick-thinking men like Cruzatte and Floyd keep the boat from being dashed to pieces.

One day we hit a spot called "Devil's Race." The river was mighty fierce, and we near lost the keelboat! It got caught on a sand bar with the river smashing against it. It tilted up and started to flip. Some of the men scrambled to put weight on the high side while others grabbed towropes and jumped into the water. Suddenly we heard a loud crack and someone yelled, "Watch out, Cruzatte!"

We saw the heavy mast and its sail start to fall. Cruzatte stood directly beneath it, struggling to bring the boat about with an oar. He looked up and dived out of the way just as the mast hit the deck. Whew! That was a close one!

Without the wind pulling at the sail, we finally got the boat righted. From shore, the swimmers used the towropes to pull us out of danger. When the crew could relax, they started talking about Cruzatte and his near miss.

Sergeant Floyd asked, "Who yelled, anyway?"

"It was Paul Hale, the captains' young assistant," answered one of the Fields brothers.

"If that don't beat all," said Gass. "That kid's got sharp eyes. Quick too. Why, reminds me of that little sparrow hawk you spotted yesterday, Captain Lewis."

"That's a right fitting name for the youngster, if you ask me," said Floyd.

Everyone agreed, including Paul. From that point on he answered to "Sparrow Hawk."

Our relief at getting through Devil's Race only lasted until we checked for damages. We needed to stop and make repairs. Lewis sent out a couple of men to find the right trees for making a mast and more oars. Most of ours had been smashed from fighting the current. Sparrow Hawk helped weave new towropes from hide strips.

Later, Joe Fields killed an animal the Frenchmen call a "barrow." He held it up for us to see. "It looks something like a beaver, but it's a sight meaner. And it carries its body just high enough to clear the ground."

Checking out the inch-long claws on its front paws, I figured it was no animal to tangle with.

The mosquitoes and gnats are thicker here than feathers in a down quilt! It's a trial swatting at them while I work on my map of the river for President Jefferson. Hot weather adds to the misery. As usual, old McNeal complains the loudest. Back in our winter camp outside St. Louis, he'd go on about the cold. Now he's saying, "I tell ya, it's so hot we could fry up supper on one of them flat rocks — that is, if the skeeters didn't eat the meat first."

We are constantly digging through Dr. Rush's medical box to treat dysentery and those sunstruck from working in the 100 degree heat. No one got too sick except Sergeant Floyd. Nothing seemed to help him. He tried to work, but he couldn't keep any food or water down. We knew he wasn't long for this world. But he fought it hard, and his mind stayed strong to the end. He died on August 22. We buried him on top of a bluff by a small river we named for him. No one said much, but I figure we were all asking ourselves, *Who'll be next?*

Even though we left that bluff a ways back, our question still tends to nag at us. We see Indian war parties on the river banks 'most every day now. So far when we come ashore, they've been friendly enough. But they warn us about a hostile tribe: "Sioux upriver. They rob. They kill."

President Jefferson wants to make peace with this tribe — I hope they're willing!

CAPTAIN WILLIAM CLARK

Chapter Two
ARROWS, RIFLES, AND A CANNON

Fort Mandan, March 19, 1805

Watching the ice chunks swirl away in the flooded Missouri reminds me it will soon be time to leave this fort and continue west. But most of the soldiers won't be going with us. The president told them to return to St. Louis after getting us through the first sixteen hundred miles of our journey. Just this morning, our interpreter, George Drouillard, said, "I'm going to miss those men, Captain. Their added strength saved our hides back with them Teton Sioux."

How well I know! More than once, only our show of force saved us. One time Chief Black Buffalo invited a few of us to visit their village during peace talks. As soon as Clark and some others got off the boat, his braves surrounded them. Clark drew his sword, and his men took aim. On the boat, I shouted orders to the rest of our crew. "Take up your rifles and put an Indian in your sights. Sergeant Gass, prepare the cannon. Fire on my command!"

Three warriors notched their arrows for every one of our men with rifles. Clark told me later, "I'd had it with their threats, trickery, and scare tactics. I was feeling like bear fat in a hot skillet, and I meant it when I said we'd shoot if they didn't back off." And they did back off, after some long, tension-filled moments.

The Sioux continued to be a constant danger, even after we stopped for winter. Outside a Mandan Indian village, we built this fort to hold up in through winter. One day when two of our men were out hunting, a war party attacked and took their horses. They told us, "The Indians got to arguing about us. That's when we lit out!"

I took twenty-four men and some Mandans to go after our horses. But the Sioux had too big a lead, and we ended up hunting for meat, not men. We got back to the fort with thirty-six elk and fourteen deer.

Except for the Sioux, our dealings with the Indians have gone well. We have now signed treaties with the Omaha, Oto, Missouri, Mandan, Minnetaree, and Arikara. After smoking the peace pipe, giving gifts, and talking, the chiefs have accepted President Jefferson's peace plan.

Drouillard is wary about their acceptance of the peace terms. One day he pulled me aside and said, "Captain, I'm thinking the Indians don't understand these peace treaties. You talk about the United States owning the land. That's not the Indians' way."

Only time will tell if our scout is right.

Our medals, needles, mirrors, and other gifts pleased the natives. So does York's dancing. He amazes all the tribes. Most have never seen black skin. They crowd around, examining him. But he does not mind, and even puts on a show. "Me, wild people-eater," he says with a big grin while lifting a heavy rock to show his powerful muscles. Then Cruzatte plays his fiddle, and York starts dancing, jumping, and twisting in all directions.

"Captain, look at those Indians stare," said one of the Fields brothers. "If we ever run into another war party, just put York out front. After a minute of his wild footwork, we'll be able to walk up and take their weapons right out of their hands."

Besides getting to know the Indians, we've met some trappers — many from the Northwest Trading Company. They want to know about the Louisiana Purchase. From their questions, I suspect they also want to know why we are going west.

I usually let Clark handle these buckskin-clad Englishmen. He does better than I. One of our men expressed my feelings when he said, "It goes against my grain, talking all friendly with them redcoats. They killed my kin and neighbors in the Revolution."

We have hired other trappers to go west with us since we are losing the soldiers. But the new men neither read nor write, and some can't even swim. One Frenchman name Charbonneau has a Shoshone woman, captured from a tribe west of here. He calls her Sacajawea. She just gave birth to a baby boy. If not for her, we'd leave the difficult Charbonneau behind. She knows the languages of the Rocky Mountain tribes, and Drouillard only knows the talk of the Missouri ones. We'll need her to interpret for us.

Though we face the unknown, many of the men figure the months ahead can't be much worse than the winter here. We had miserable cold spells. One morning we woke up to a temperature of forty degrees below zero and trees covered with ice. Some days we couldn't hunt, and many of the men suffered from frostbite. Once McNeal's cold hands let his ax slip, and he cut his leg. While I doctored it, he said, "I tell you, Captain, only these here sod huts we built stand between us and a frozen grave. It's a wonder I even knew I cut myself, with the cold making me so numb."

Even the great Missouri River froze. That's when our boats got trapped. Clark and I feared the expanding ice would crush them, so we set the men to cutting them out. It didn't work — nothing worked. We heated rocks, but they exploded! We heated iron stakes and drove them into the ice. The frozen water barely cracked! And we rigged a pulley, but our elk-hide ropes broke. Almost a month later when the ice began to thaw, we finally got our crafts free. Now they're ready for travel.

The soldiers will take the big keelboat back to St. Louis while the rest of us take smaller boats upriver. What lies before us no one knows. But the Indians keep warning us about white bears, saying, "Very fierce. Very big. No kill easy. You die if you not watch for."

Even with the threat of bears, excitement fills us. Unknown land waits ahead.

CAPTAIN MERIWETHER LEWIS

Chapter Three

GRIZZLY BEARS!

On the Missouri River, Past Great Falls, August 1, 1805

I'm thirty-five years old today. The jerked meat I'm gnawing on hardly makes for a party, but at least we're not fighting bears, wind, buffalo, or cactus. Since leaving Fort Mandan, there's been a heap of close shaves, and we're all getting mighty raw.

The first "white" bear I saw charged me! Even after I wounded him! I'd be a pile of bones right now if my gunshot hadn't slowed the brute down, allowing me to reload and shoot again. Actually, the bear wasn't white. He had dark fur with whitish specks on the ends of the hairs, making him look grizzled.

No matter the color, the second bear gave real meaning to the Mandans' warning. George Drouillard and I ran into it while hunting. The grizzly took ten of our shots, roaring all the while!

"I don't believe it, Captain!" shouted Drouillard. "That bear still ain't down. It's heading for a sand bar in the river."

We gathered more men and followed the trail.

When we caught up with it, the bear was dead. We measured him at eight feet, seven and a half inches, with claws longer than most men's fingers!

While we were eating bear steaks that night, the crew got to talking about tackling the critters. Sergeant Gass said, "Nature's made them the hunters. The less we meet up with them, the better off we'll be. Even the dog steers clear."

Some of the men nodded, saying amen. But Colter said, "I don't agree. The test of hunting so fierce a beast makes me want to pack up my rifle and head out right now."

Colter got his wish the next morning. McNeal spotted a grizzly sleeping in the open. "We need meat, so now is our chance," Colter told Whitehouse and the Fields brothers. "The four of us will get close and shoot. Two others need to hold back. If our four shots don't take the brute down, they'll finish him off."

The plan seemed a good one, but it didn't work! The animal took all six shots and charged. The men ran for the river. One jumped into a canoe while the others took to the willows. The Fields reloaded and fired again. Their noise turned the giant toward them, and they jumped into the river. The angry bear went right in after them, teeth bared and roaring. Whitehouse shot the beast in the head just in time to save the two brothers.

The bears provided danger aplenty, but strong winds caused us even more trouble. The gusts whipped up waves that kept our boats swamped for days. Then a sudden squall hit, and Charbonneau panicked. He let go of the rudder and closed his eyes. "*Mon Dieu, save us!*"

The boat tipped on its side. Our instruments, journals and some trade goods spilled into the river. The crew was hanging on for their lives. Cruzatte whipped out his pistol and pointed it at Charbonneau. "Grab that rudder, *monsieur* and turn this boat toward shore, or I'll put a hole in ya."

Looking down the barrel of the gun, the Frenchman grabbed the rudder. The boat slowly straightened up and limped to shore.

Thanks to Sacajawea, we didn't lose much. In the midst of the trouble, she fished out our journals and instruments from the water. The scientific part of our expedition would have ended if it hadn't been for her quick action. To honor her, we called an uncharted river "Bird Woman River," after the meaning of her name.

Our troubles were far from over. A few days later Lewis and I woke up to a gunshot. We heard someone yell, "Watch out! Buffalo in camp!"

While scrambling in our tent, the ground under us set to shaking. Scannon started barking something fierce as heavy hooves thundered past.

Sparrow Hawk came running up as we got out of our tent. "Captains, you all right? We thought you were goners for sure! Scannon saved you."

"That bull must've been crazy," one man said, pointing at two scattered campfires. "He charged out of the dark like his tail was on fire. I only got one shot off as he headed straight for your tent. Scannon took to his heels, barking like a mad dog. He turned that old bull and headed him out of camp."

I reached down and gave Lewis's dog a good scratch. That night I was plumb grateful he was with us. I told Lewis, "It's a good thing you didn't sell Scannon to those Indians who wanted to trade beaver pelts for your 'tame bear'."

After that, things settled down for a few days. Then we heard a mighty roaring upriver. We paddled to shore and walked a ways ahead. "No man will go over those falls and live to tell about it," Cruzatte said.

Looking at the huge wall of water, none of us doubted him. We took off carrying our canoes around the Great Falls. We wore out our moccasins in no time, as the rough land and never-ending prickly-pear cactus chewed up every leather sole we sewed. With sore feet and the loaded canoes, it took fourteen days to go sixteen miles.

One day, a hailstorm hit us. York, Sacajawea, Charbonneau, and I were out scouting when the ice started flying. "Head for that ravine," I yelled.

We held up under an overhanging rock. By the time we reached the shelter, we all had bloody gashes from the sharp ice. Then rain started pouring down, and we heard a sound like thunder in the distance. York looked at me. "That don't sound like sky thunder."

York set his hands on the edge of the rock above us and heaved himself over it. Then he helped the rest of us climb up. I came last, just as a mighty rush of river hit our overhang! I just missed getting swept away as the flash flood tore through the ravine.

After going through all this, I can't complain none about eating jerky on my birthday — at least I'm here to celebrate it. But I don't know about my thirty-sixth. The snow capped Rockies lie before us. We need horses and food. Except for the wounded deer Scannon hauled out of the river, fresh meat is mighty scarce. We hope to find Sacajawea's people soon. We're going to need all the help we can get before crossing those mountains!

CAPTAIN WILLIAM CLARK

Chapter Four
A CAPTIVE RETURNS HOME

Nez Perce Camp, West of the Rocky Mountains, September 24, 1805

President Jefferson thought we could cross the Rocky Mountains in one day. Little did he, Clark, or I know how endless these rugged peaks would be. Without the help of Indians, we would never have made it across at all.

The first sign that help was close came when Sacajawea stopped and pointed toward a high rock. "Beaver's Head. We get close to my people."

Hearing her words, Clark and I felt relief. We needed horses and information about other rivers that went west. The Missouri had been getting harder to travel every day. Often we had to drag the boats through shallow waters. And when we hit deeper places, rapids forced us to use towropes. Thorny bushes grew along the shore, so we had to wade into the water to haul the boats. We cut our feet and fell on the slippery rocks. More than once canoes flipped over. We even lost a spare gun and some shot.

Because of the rough going, it was decided that I should take some men and go ahead to find the Shoshone. First we found rattlesnakes! Hundreds of them. Shields asked me, "Captain, you ever seen so many rattlers in all your born days?"

I never had. We'd been plagued by these poisonous snakes all along this stretch of the Missouri. Many in our expedition heard rattles just in time to jump back and avoid fangs. But nothing prepared us for these cliffs. Every ledge and exposed rock had one or more rattlers curled up on it. I named the place "Rattlesnake Cliffs."

Continuing on, we found an ice-cold stream bubbling out of the ground at the base of a low mountain. After more than a year of grueling days and restless nights, we'd reached the beginning of the Missouri!

Drouillard shook his head. "It just don't hardly seem possible that this little stream turns into the mighty Missouri!"

McNeal felt the wonder of it, too. He put his feet on each side of the stream. Then he raised his face to heaven and said, "Thank ya, God, for letting me live to straddle a river I thought had no end."

A little farther on, our group found the Shoshone. They greeted us with cheek-to-cheek, one-armed hugs. After getting smeared with paint and grease by sixty Shoshone warriors, I was heartily tired of their tribal hug.

At first they didn't believe we were white men. Our skin was as brown as theirs, and our long hair had not seen a comb in months. A feather stuck out from my hat, and my hide shirt looked like theirs. Finally, I pulled up my sleeve to show them my white skin.

By sign language, we let the chief know that we needed to return to the rest of our company. They went back with us. When we got close to Clark's party, Sacajawea started dancing and sucking her fingers. "That shows she is one of their tribe," her husband told us.

Cameahwait, the chief, approached her. She wept and threw her blanket around him. We found out that he is her brother! Then other family and friends greeted her.

We enjoyed our stay at their camp. Sparrow Hawk even fished with the tribe. They caught 528 trout! When I asked our assistant how he did it, he said, "It was York's idea. He said servants in Virginia often used nets made from bushes. We used the nets to trap the fish, then we just waded out and tossed them to the Indian women on shore."

Our trading didn't go as well as our fishing. We only got twelve horses. The chief said Minnetaree raids left them with only a few extras. "But ahead you meet Nez Perce. They own many horses. You trade. Get more."

Before tackling the Rockies on foot, we loaded our canoes with rocks and sank them in a nearby pond for safekeeping. Sacajawea said good-bye to her people. They invited her to stay, but she decided to go with us.

The mountain travel was hard even after we traded for twenty-eight more horses with a tribe of Flathead Indians. For every peak we crossed, another rose before us. We slouched in our saddles and talked little. I watched Sacajawea carry her son and wondered if she wished she'd stayed with her tribe.

Hunting proved poor too. Drouillard told us, "There just ain't much game this high up." Finally we had to butcher one of our horses.

"This meat ain't half bad," Sergeant Gass said.

McNeal chewed another bite. "Shoot, we're so hungry, porcupine quills would taste good."

We satisfied our hunger for the moment, but things continued to get worse. Fallen timbers and thick brush constantly blocked the steep trail. Both horse and man risked broken legs with every step. Two pack animals even fell backward.

The higher we went, the colder it grew. Snow forced the crew to wrap their feet in rags before putting on their moccasins. "I'm not sure why I'm doing this," a man said one day. "By noon, my feet are so numb, I wouldn't know if they fell off my legs."

Clark went ahead to build warming fires. It was not enough. After talking, we decided he must push on to seek help and find an end to these vast mountains. A few days later he returned with some Nez Perce Indians. We could not have lasted much longer. Our strength and food were gone.

The tribe's dried fish and roots looked like manna from heaven. We feasted, only to have the heavily salted food make our weak bodies sick. I could barely sit a horse on the way to their village. Others had to lie down alongside the trail.

Judging by the shape we're in, we should not leave this camp for a time. But we must not delay. The chiefs tell us, "Rivers to the west. You paddle to big waters."

I think of our weak condition and the canoes we must build. The trees are already bright with fall colors. Can we make it to the Pacific before winter closes in on us?

CAPTAIN MERIWETHER LEWIS

Chapter Five

CRUZATTE PROVES HIS WORTH

Pacific Coast, December 5, 1805

Between the constant rain and Lewis not getting back from scouting for a winter campsite, I've been tighter than a string on Cruzatte's fiddle. I needed something to keep busy, and that's when Sparrow Hawk suggested making a marker to show our arrival. "If Daniel Boone did it to record the killing of a bear, we ought to do it to record the crossing of a whole continent!"

Sitting by the fire today, I can view my handiwork. Even the sheets of rain don't hide the fresh carving on the tree. *William Clark December 3rd 1805. By land from the U. States in 1804 & 1805.*

Reading my words, I think of the tough time we just went through. I reckon we'd all have died without ol' Cruzatte. His skills as a boatman sure saved our hides more than once.

After leaving the Nez Perce camp, we went through a regular puzzle of streams, finally ending up on the Columbia River. At first things weren't too bad, and we even traded with some Yakimas. This tribe spoke the Nez Perce language, but they lived more like other Columbia River tribes, except they dressed fancier. They love white. Their elk skins are decorated with sea shells, and they use white buffalo robes! Yet, in spite of their grand appearance, every day is a struggle for them to get enough food.

We ate our first dog with them. Sparrow Hawk couldn't stand to do it. He looked at Scannon and pushed away a stick with roasted meat on it. "There's no way I'm going to eat a dog." Instead the youngster choked down more roots and dried fish.

Back on the river, we hit other waterfalls. After Cruzatte and I scouted the land, we used elk-hide ropes to lower our boats over a cliff. The crew carried them around to the shore. Trudging through the sand, the men started slapping their legs and rubbing their arms. Someone cried out, "Ouch, something bit me!"

"A whole bunch of something," added Drouillard.

"Fleas!" said George Shannon. "I'm covered with them. I've got to get them off before I go crazy with itching." The lot of us stripped and brushed ourselves down, but more of the pests took their place.

We figured they were swarming around because of all the dead and dried fish. The river Indians made great piles of the stuff, mainly salmon. They even dry and stretch the salmon skins to make baskets to carry the fish. They say they use the dried fish to trade with white men on ships. In exchange, they receive copper and metal pots, jackets, and blue beads. Exposure to white men has not improved the Indians. They steal and threaten. Lewis and I are certain Sacajawea's pres-

ence keeps them from attacking. Indians believe that a woman on a trip means the journey's purpose is peaceful.

The Columbia River sure wasn't peaceful! It plunged over falls and poured into narrow gorges. Between stony ledges, the water pitched into great waves and crashed onto rocks. The churning water left foam floating everywhere. But somehow Cruzatte got us through. For a week we ran water that looked impossible. Then we hit the biggest gorge I've ever seen! It looked like we were going to have to ditch our canoes and walk to the Pacific.

"Captain Clark," Cruzatte said, "I think we can do it. We'll make the runs two at a time, so if one of us gets in trouble, the other can help out. It'll take

a few trips to get all the boats through, but at least we won't be walking!"

Run after run, the Frenchman and I battled the churning water. Dodging rocks and folding into waves, we paddled for our lives. Even the Indians watched us from the cliffs above. At one point, my canoe turned sideways and a huge wave tipped it. I was ready to take my chances in the water when Cruzatte yelled, "Hold steady, Captain! The next wave should push you up again." God bless the man; he was right!

That night, Cruzatte got his fiddle out, and the crew set to dancing. I even got my toes tapping for a tune or two. We needed it after those six days! But our dancing didn't last. It started raining and just never let up. We got trapped on a beach! Cruzatte broke the news. "The rain and the high waves push us back on shore. We can't get through."

"My news ain't any better," reported Gass. "The underbrush around us is as thick as those fleas upriver. There's no way we can haul our supplies and canoes through it without cutting miles of trail."

Our camp was more often than not floating in shallow water, but we couldn't hunt, go back, or move forward. New dangers came with every toss of the waves.

One night Scannon woke us with his barking.

Looking to see what upset him, we spotted a two-hundred-foot drift log hurling our way. York and Potts scrambled away just as the trunk rolled over where they'd been sleeping. The thing measured more than seven feet in diameter!

"Captain Lewis, your dog saved me from becoming a flapjack, and I'm real grateful," said York.

Pummeled by the weather, we dodged drift logs and flooding for a week before the rains stopped. Loading up supplies, Shields said, "I feel kinda like that barking squirrel we got back on the prairie. It held up in its hole while we tried to shoot, dig, and flood it out. When we finally added the critter to our specimen box, it was mighty bedraggled and soaking wet!"

Shield wasn't far off about the way we looked. It felt awfully good when the sun came out a few days later. But now it's raining again. I'm sitting by this hissing fire, fearful for Lewis. He's crossed the mouth of the Columbia, scouting to the south. This place is a maze of dead-end streams and ocean-crashing waves. The natives still aren't real friendly either. We need shelter and food. We need Lewis to make it back safe!

CAPTAIN WILLIAM CLARK

Chapter Six

ESCAPE FROM FORT MISERABLE

Hot Springs, Eastern Rockies, June 30, 1806

What a change! These hot springs are soaking out the months of Fort Clatsop's dampness and cold. We're finally heading east — heading home.

I'd had high hopes for the winter camp I found on the coast, although locating it took longer than I expected. I'll never forget the relief on Clark's face when I returned.

Once we all got to the campsite, it rained the whole time we built our cabins. The damp rotted our clothes off and chilled every man to the bone. When we finally finished, Colter suggested, "How about calling the place Fort Clatsop, after a tribe around here? We did that last winter at Fort Mandan, and it proved real lucky."

Our luck did not hold. Hordes of fleas took over the cabins, whose roofs sprang leaks every day. Without chimneys, the smoke made our eyes burn and set us to coughing. Keeping food was a trial

also. The elk and deer we killed spoiled in the wet weather. Often we had to eat roots and fish. We did make salt from sea water, which improved the taste of the poor food.

One afternoon the men from our salt pit ran into the fort. "An Indian tried to murder me," McNeal gasped. As we gathered around, he continued, "He acted real friendly and said he had a good white man's shirt for trade in his hut. I went with him, not suspecting anything. I didn't pay no mind to the squaws that started hollering."

"You never heard such a ruckus," Colter said. "The women kept pointing at the hut Hugh had gone into. Joe and I pulled the flap back and saw a brave ready to stab Hugh while he was looking at a sailor's jacket. We jumped him right quick."

Besides the hostile Indians, sickness tormented us. Sore throats, coughs, fevers, and aching joints bothered every crew member. No doubt the damp

caused it. In the end, our misery led us to leave the Pacific coast two weeks earlier than planned.

Our time at Fort Clatsop proved to be the worst of the expedition so far. It rained for all but twelve days, and the sun shone only three. We killed 150 elk, twenty deer, lots of ducks, and even a raccoon, yet still struggled for food. We did manage to eat three meals a day, but nobody is keeping the recipes!

Our start was risky because we lacked supplies. We only had candlefish. These foot-long, gray fish had just left the ocean and headed up the Columbia. We netted hundreds of them. Sparrow Hawk asked a Chinook brave about the name. "We dry. Set on fire in dark huts. Give much light. Last long, like white man's candle."

That was the last friendly meeting we had with the coast Indians. A short time later John Shields stayed behind to trade for a dog. When he caught up, he told us, "Indians attacked me." Catching his breath, he added, "After getting the dog, I headed out to catch up with you. But on the trail, some braves blocked my way. They pushed me aside and tried to take my new dog and pack. I pulled my knife. They lit out, and I didn't wait around to see if they'd come back with friends!"

A few days later other Indians took Scannon. Three of our crew caught up with the scoundrels on the trail. Our anger must have shown because right away they untied the rope from my dog's neck and gave him back.

Amid all this trouble, we kept trying to trade for horses to travel overland. Winter storms and spring runoff raised the level of the river twelve feet! No one could paddle against its raging current. But horse-trading with the river Indians tried our patience. The braves stole, threw rocks, backed down on trades, and tried to scare us.

We left with only four horses. While carrying our two loaded canoes, we trudged through deep sand and climbed over jagged rocks. But it was worth it to reach the Nez Perce camp. These natives were honest and helpful. They restored our faith in the Indians.

When we talked of going east, they warned us, "No go through Rocky Mountains. Much snow."

The warning did not set well. "What I wouldn't give to see home again," the men groaned.

After staying with this tribe for six weeks, we tried the pass. The trip didn't last long. "We can't make it," Drouillard said while pulling his elk robe tighter. "Snow hides the trail, and we don't have enough food to make it if we get lost. We need a guide."

We headed back down the steep trail. Then Colter's horse slipped. Both horse and rider splashed into the creek beside us. The flooded rapids carried them downstream, tumbling them over each other. Someone spotted them and yelled, "Colter's caught a limb!"

Farther down, his horse found some footing. We expected the worst, but they got away with only bruises from their wild ride.

We went just halfway back down the mountain to a meadow. I sent two men to the village for a guide. They came back with half the tribe!

The next morning we tried the trail again with two braves leading us. The frozen pass whipped up a wind that slipped in and around our fur robes. The steep ups and downs set our muscles to quivering. The horses searched for grass but couldn't find any. We ate bear grease and roots. But in truth, it went better than we thought. A hard crust topped the snow, allowing our horses to walk over the fallen timbers and rocks that troubled us last fall. After 150 miles and seven long, hard days, we made it!

Below the snow line, we found these hot springs, and each of us feels comfort in the warm water. But the break is only temporary.

Clark and I have decided to split up. We must see if another river goes west. Neither of us wants to face unknown land and Indians with divided forces. But the president wants to know if there's a waterway to the Pacific. I just hope we make it back to tell him the answer!

CAPTAIN MERIWETHER LEWIS

Chapter Seven

BATTLES WITH THE BLACKFEET

Missouri River, east of Yellowstone River, August 12, 1806

Lewis's pale face and feverish sleep set me to worrying and thinking. How could my friend make it through a horse fall, near drowning, more grizzlies, and an Indian attack only to end up shot by an unidentified man?

We rest now, and I'm taking down Lewis's story in the journal since he can't write it for himself.

The tale begins when we split up at the hot springs. Lewis had just started off with his ten men to explore the Marias River off north when Sparrow Hawk yelled, "Captain Clark, look!"

What I saw near stopped my breathing. Lewis and his horse were sprawled at the bottom of a steep rocky slope. Someone said that he saw Lewis's horse slip on the mountainside, sending them tumbling over rocks, logs, and brush. The horse came within a hair's width of rolling on top of Lewis. Somehow they both got up unhurt!

A few days later, Lewis's party hit a flooded stream. They had to build a raft for their supplies and for the men who couldn't swim. On the last trip across, a swift current sent the Fields brothers and Lewis into rough water. For over a mile they dodged rocks and fought the waves. Finally they started pulling toward shore, when they realized they were sinking!

They lost control of the raft again, slipping back into the current. Suddenly a low branch knocked Lewis into the water. With less weight, the raft rose. The Fields brothers gradually steered the raft back to the edge while the captain swam for shore. All made it — wet but safe.

McNeal also came close to dying. He returned to Lewis's camp at the day's end with a hair-raising story and a busted rifle. "I was doing what you asked, Captain — just riding along the river to dig up the supplies we buried last fall. Then all of a sudden a grizzly steps out of the thick brush not ten

feet from me. My horse reared, tossing me right at the bear's feet. It rose on its hind legs, all set to have me for dinner.

"Thought I was a goner, being too close to shoot. But my pap didn't raise no quitter, so I got up and whacked that bear over the head with my rifle. Knocked him clean over. While he lay there, pawing his head, I hot-footed it to the nearest tree.

"When that ol' grizzly got up, he was madder than a riled hornet's nest. He came at my tree roaring, clawing, and pacing around it. Stayed there for more than two hours. I don't mind telling you, I clean near jumped for joy when he lumbered off."

Lewis later told me, "I suspect McNeal's story will get bigger and better with each telling. But even so, I'd rather face two Indians on the warpath than one grizzly."

Lewis later sent six of his men to carry supplies around the Great Falls. They were aiming to meet men from my party who'd picked up our sunken canoes. Then they'd all go down the Missouri, and our whole group would join up. Anyhow, Lewis headed out overland with only Drouillard and the Fields brothers.

Within days they saw that the Marias River didn't go west. They turned their tails back toward the Missouri, only to run smack into a Blackfeet war party. The braves looked like they were making to attack at first, but then they acted friendly, inviting the men to camp with them. Lewis didn't like the idea, but he knew their horses were too tuckered out to make a run for it. Later he talked of peace. They said nothing. That night he set up guard shifts among the four of them.

Joe Fields fell asleep at his post, but lucky for us Drouillard woke up when something tugged at his rifle. A brave stood over him with his hands on ol' George's gun. Drouillard yanked his firearm and yelled, "Let go of my gun!"

The rest of the men woke with a start and grabbed for their rifles. They were gone! Other

Blackfeet warriors had them. Lewis drew his pistol, and Reuben Fields pulled out his knife.

A ruckus followed, and then the Indians went after the horses and started shooting. They missed, but Lewis and Drouillard did not. In the end, the Indians left.

"This ain't over," Drouillard said. "They'll be back with others for revenge."

Our men took off. They rode for miles on end, stopping only twice in sixteen hours to eat and feed the horses. Finally they had to lie down for some shuteye. They woke up so sore they could hardly walk but pressed on to the Missouri and the waiting canoes.

After meeting up with the other men, Lewis pushed downriver, trying to put a lot of miles between them and the Blackfeet. He took no pleasure in the fact that after five thousand miles, they'd been forced to kill their first Indians.

When a large herd of elk appeared on shore, Sergeant Gass said, "Captain, you got to let the men rest. And we need meat too."

Lewis called a halt, letting the rest of the men take it easy while he and Cruzatte went hunting. They killed one animal and were tracking another one when Lewis heard the crack of a rifle. A second later he felt a hot jab of pain in his thigh. Right off

he figured his poor-sighted hunting companion had mistaken his elk-skin clothes and shot him. Cruzatte admitted shooting but just couldn't say he'd shot the captain. "I tell ya, it was an elk."

My travels sound pretty tame after what Lewis went through. While he was out cheating death time and again, I went out along the Yellowstone River. We had our trials — wet river crossings, tormenting mosquitoes, and even getting our horses stolen — but now it all seems kinda mild. We do miss our horses, especially the spotted Appaloosas that the Nez Perce gave us. But we're mighty glad the Indians were more interested in our horses than our hides.

I'm going to be sorry to tell Lewis about what's ahead. He doesn't look too good right now. But when he wakes up, I'll have to report what the two trappers said when they stopped by our camp a few days ago: "The tribes along the upper Missouri are fighting again. Lots of war parties are out, and it's risky traveling. We snuck through, but the Indians ain't likely to miss all you folks heading back to St. Louis."

CAPTAIN WILLIAM CLARK

Chapter Eight
BACK FROM THE DEAD

St. Louis, Missouri, September 25, 1806

I have recovered from my gunshot wound, and now I must again take pen in hand to continue these journals.

During the last part of our journey, we made good speed going down the Missouri. In one day we passed six of last year's upriver camps! War parties did not trouble us coming back to Fort Mandan, but we found our buildings a pile of ashes. Then we talked with the tribes. Yes, the Indians were back at war with each other.

My injury limited what I could do, but as often as possible I joined in councils with the chiefs. We spoke strongly against war. Each Missouri tribe said the Sioux were a bad influence. We told them to have nothing to do with this trouble-making tribe.

One Arikara chief said, "We understand. No more fight. No more Sioux — but one last trade with them." He wanted to trade extra horses for guns!

Clark summed up our feelings when he said, "Talking peace with these tribes leaves me feeling as frustrated as an eggless hen!" At least we got Big White Chief to come with us to meet President Jefferson.

Though we gained the Mandan chief, we lost other members of our company. Colter left to join a trapping expedition that was heading west again. When he left, he told Shannon, "I'll think of you when I'm boiling meat in them hot springs we found by the Yellowstone."

Shannon waved and said, "I'll think of you when I'm eating my sister's fried chicken and apple pie!"

Charbonneau, Sacajawea, and her son, Little Pomp, left too. Clark became quite attached to the boy and offered Charbonneau a job in St. Louis. The Frenchman refused. Then my friend said, "Will you let me raise the boy? He's half white, and I'll see he gets a good education." In the end, Sacajawea promised to bring her son to Clark next year.

Heading back downriver, we ran into our old Sioux enemies. The first sign of trouble came when we spotted a few Indians on shore, waving and acting friendly. We took no chances and kept to the middle of the river since the tribes were warring. The next thing we knew, ninety armed braves lined the ridge!

We pulled up on the opposite bank. A group of warriors swam across. That's when we realized they were Sioux. Clark had Drouillard tell them, "We remember your ways. You treated us badly two years ago. I had to draw my sword. We want no part of you. Go now, or we'll shoot."

The braves swam back, and we took off down river. We made camp on a sand bar but worried about the Fieldes and Shannon. They had left the boats earlier to do some hunting. Now they would have to pass the warriors to rejoin us.

Unaware of the danger, the hunting party paddled upriver. As good fortune would have it, the braves had left the shore. Our hunters made it safely to camp, only to have Nature break loose. About midnight, a hard rain and strong wind blew away our canoes. Two ended up clear across the river. After collecting our boats and supplies, we slept only a little. Mosquitoes woke us up bright and early.

The next people we ran into were white men — one a good friend of Clark's, by the name of Robert McClellan. With some soldiers, he was going to the Arikaras. A chief of theirs had gone to Washington and had died. I did not envy McClellan facing the tribe with such poor news.

Speaking of news, we could hardly believe what McClellan told us.

"People think all of you are dead! There were all kinds of stories about your expedition — they said you were lost, that you were killed, even that you ended up as prisoners in the Spanish mines. No one thought you'd ever return."

We got more news from home as we passed other travelers heading upriver.

"Imagine that," Sergeant Gass said. "Burr shot old Alex Hamilton!"

"What gets me," said Shannon, "is the British firing on a ship in New York Harbor! We licked them redcoats once, and we'll do it again if we have to."

Although the crew wanted nothing more than to reach home, we stopped to visit Sergeant Floyd's grave on the bluff overlooking the river that bore his name. It had been opened, but we made it proper again. As we shared a moment of silence, I suspect we thought the same thing. *Will this honorable man be the only one of us who dies on the Corps of Discovery?*

Back in our canoes, the men wanted to keep going, not even stopping to hunt.

"We'll make do with leftover biscuits," Pryor said.

A day's journey out of St. Louis, people lined the banks of the river, shouting and firing their rifles. Truly they thought we had come back from the dead! No sooner did we set foot on shore than a dozen people asked, "Won't you come to supper?" We took their invitations kindly. After eating horse heads, ravens, rotten fish, and dog meat, the taste of a home-cooked meal was just shy of heaven!

At this moment, however, I find that "civilization" is uncomfortable. A starched white shirt chafes my neck, and new boots squeeze my feet. To think I must dance in these tonight!

I remember the last ball I dressed for. Was it really more than two years ago? Yes, and the wilderness has surely left its mark on me. Though I will get used to the starch and boots, I will never forget the softness of a doe's hide or the comfort of good moccasins.

I have many other thoughts running through my head. I think of the Corps of Discovery ending with the frenzied welcome of the St. Louis crowds. I think of Sergeant Floyd, Little Pomp, James Colter, and Sparrow Hawk. I think of this great land we call the United States. Even as I join others on the ballroom floor tonight, I know I won't be able to resist telling of our incredible journey — of the roar of the Pacific, the vast heights of the Rocky Mountains and the power of the mighty Missouri River.

CAPTAIN MERIWETHER LEWIS

Epilogue

A LETTER FROM CLARK

St. Louis, Missouri, January 1, 1823

Dear Sparrow Hawk,

What a surprise to get your letter after so many years of wondering what happened to you! Imagine, you getting a college education and becoming a doctor! I've not forgotten what an observant and helpful assistant you were as we traveled over six thousand miles with President Jefferson's Corps of Discovery. Much has happened since that journey, and I would share the news of those who traveled with us.

First I must tell you a hard thing. Captain Lewis is dead. He died on October 11, 1809, while on a trip to Washington. Though he lived only thirty-five years, we must never forget that Meriwether Lewis experienced more on our journey west than most people do in a lifetime. I will always remember this excellent friend.

With the worst news behind, I can go on to share what I know of the other members of our expedition. Shannon lost a leg when the Arikaras shot him while helping return Big White Chief to his people. The accident slowed the man about as much as a log stops a beaver! First he got Lewis's and my journals ready for publication, and then he started studying law. Before I knew it, word came down that he was a senator and circuit judge.

McNeal and Willard re-enlisted in the army. I understand they each married and raised large families. I couldn't help smiling when I heard Willard named two of his sons Lewis and Clark! He also wrote of making plans to take his family out west by wagon train. He wants to settle in California.

Colter and Drouillard headed back into the areas we explored. It grieved me to learn the Blackfeet killed Drouillard. They must have surprised ol' George because a finer shot couldn't be found anywhere. But Colter still lives. He explored the Yellowstone. There's talk of naming the area after the river. A few even speak of protecting this wilderness by making a national park.

There's also news that directly concerns you. A year after we returned, Congress gave each of us 320 acres west of the Mississippi. Ordway turned into a farmer, but others, like you, never claimed the land. Gass sold his. You know he's pushing sixty and courting some gal. It wouldn't surprise me if he had a bunch of kids and outlived us all!

York is no longer my slave. I freed him and gave him a wagon with six horses. He set up a freight business, but former slaves struggle much in these times. People still think of them as servants. I guess sometimes I do too, even though I know better. York was equal to any person on our journey — in working, in playing, and in caring for others. But it's hard to change a lifetime of thinking.

To tell my story, I must tell Charbonneau's and Sacajawea's. Our lives have crossed many times since the fall of '06. I moved here to St. Louis and became the Superintendent of Indian Affairs. As she promised, Sacajawea brought me "Little Pomp," as well as his little sister Lizette. Actually I best write Jean Baptiste instead of Little Pomp. My adopted son outgrew his nickname long ago. I sent him to school, and now he leads trapping expeditions west.

As for his mother, I hear two sets of news,

neither of them good. I know she lived with the Mandan for a few years, but she either died of cholera or moved farther west without Charbonneau. On a visit, Jean tells me he has not yet found her.

Besides Sacajawea's son and daughter, I have seven of my own and three stepchildren. Though my first wife died, the Lord provided a second dear wife for me.

Some people have approached me about becoming the governor of Missouri Territory, and I believe I'll take the job. The Indians trust me, and I respect them.

As I bring this letter to a close I must tell you that I often think of the Corps of Discovery. I wonder what will become of our findings in the years that follow. Will we be forgotten? Will the trail we made cross one mighty United States someday? Will our maps and scientific work stand the test of time? Deeper still, will the different races of people ever learn to live side by side within our new country?

These questions will not be answered in my time, but I feel my life is full and has meaning. My family, my work, and my memories bring me much happiness. I am a blessed person, and I pray that you also feel the same blessing.

With Best Regards,
William Clark